New Zealand's

BACKYARD BIRDS

Ned Barraud

potton & burton

Published in 2021 by Potton & Burton
319a Hardy Street, PO Box 221,
Nelson, New Zealand
www.pottonandburton.co.nz

© Ned Barraud

Layout/typography: Floor van Lierop

ISBN 978 1 98 855030 5 (softcover)
ISBN 978 1 98 855031 2 (hardcover)
Printed in China by
Everbest Printing Co. Ltd

EVOLUTION OF BIRDS

Did you know that the birds found in your backyard have ancestors that were dinosaurs? Fossil evidence linking birds to dinosaurs first came from a small theropod called Archaeopteryx (ar-kee-op-ter-ix), 150 million years ago. This bird ancestor would have looked much like a modern bird with its wings and feathers. However, it also had claws on its wings, teeth and a long tail with vertebrae.

ALL SHAPES AND SIZES

Today, there are more than 10,000 types of birds throughout the world and they come in many different shapes and sizes. Here are a few record-breaking examples, but you won't find these in your garden.

THE WANDERING ALBATROSS
has the longest wingspan of any bird in the world, 3.5 metres, which is about the length of a small car. It can glide over the ocean for hours without flapping its wings, using the movement of the wind rising over waves to stay aloft.

THE OSTRICH
is the tallest and heaviest bird alive today. It also lays the biggest egg on record, which can weigh over 2.5 kilograms. That's more than five blocks of butter.

THE BEE HUMMINGBIRD
is the smallest living bird. It is so tiny, it weighs less than a 10 cent coin.

PARTS OF A BIRD

Most birds are built for flight. Instead of front legs or arms, they have wings. And, like a kite, to keep them in the air, their skeleton needs to be super lightweight.

BEAK/BILL The beak is the bird's tool for feeding, finding food, cleaning feathers and building a nest. The pīwakawaka has a small fine beak for picking up insects in flight, while a goldfinch has a broad strong beak for cracking open seeds. A kingfisher's beak is long and sharp for stabbing prey.

EYES Most birds have excellent vision and they generally have their eyes on the side of their head. Birds of prey, however, such as the ruru/morepork, have eyes forward-facing like ours.

EARS Birds have excellent hearing. Their ear openings are often hard to see because they don't stick out and are hidden by feathers.

BODY Birds have a light, strong skeleton with many hollow bones. A bird needs a big breastbone to support its strong muscles. These muscles are used to help flap their wings and to fly.

SMELL For most birds, smell is not as important. However, a kiwi actually has poor eyesight, so it needs a good sense of smell and touch to find worms.

WINGS The shape of the wing tells a lot about how a bird flies. A falcon has narrow V-shaped wings used for speed and diving. Pīwakawaka have short wings to hover and flutter.

down feather

tail feather

flight feather

FEATHERS All birds have feathers. Some are used for flight, while others, called down feathers, are used to keep their body warm. Feathers are made from a tough, lightweight protein called keratin – the same substance that makes up our nails and hair. Feathers can also be used to show off to a mate, to look fierce or to provide camouflage.

FEET Almost all birds have four toes with claws on the end for gripping, but the shape of the foot varies for different species and has adapted to suit what a bird needs. For example, a swimming bird has webbing between their toes to help them paddle, but a hawk has sharp talons to help them catch and kill their prey.

TAIL Stiff tail feathers help a bird to move in different directions while flying, to twist and turn, and to slow it down when it's landing.

SPRING IN THE GARDEN

Spring is the time when the garden comes back to life with bird song and a frenzy of activity. It's the right time for finding a mate, but there might be a lot of competition!

If you're up early, you'll hear the dawn chorus, when many bird species start singing together. Birds communicate with song, they sing to find a mate and to claim their territory. Some try to have the loudest voice.

You may see other ways males compete for females. These male house sparrows are fighting, but sometimes, simply strutting about looking tough is enough to impress.

Some birds use colourful and unusual plumage to attract a mate. This female California quail can't resist the male's eye-catching crest.

Sometimes a food offering is used
to impress a potential mate.
Here, a male kōtare is offering a bell
frog he's caught as a gift to the female.

...me birds do special flight displays to get
...e female's attention. The kererū flies high,
...owing off its bright white chest feathers,
...en it stalls in mid-air and plunges back down.

Once a mate is found, it's time to build a
home. This female blackbird has its beak full
of nesting material.

NESTS

A nest can keep a fragile egg safe, snug and warm. It can also help to keep chicks hidden away from predators such as rats and stoats. Nests can be very simple or very complex structures.

The female riroriro spends many weeks constructing her nest. The male doesn't help with building but he does help her collect the materials she needs, such as grass, leaves, moss and spiderweb threads, to hold it together. It is then lined with cozy down feathers.

This silvereye nest is in the shape of a cup. Many backyard birds, such as blackbirds, song thrushes and pīwakawaka, build cup-shaped nests.

A kōtare uses its strong, sharp beak to hole into a clay bank or a soft tree trunk lay its eggs. The ruru/morepork (opposi doesn't build a nest either. It finds a secr sheltered space such as the hollow in a tr trunk to raise their chicks.

Welcome swallows build their nests with beak-loads of mud, carefully layered row after row and held together with grass.

EGGS AND CHICKS

All birds lay eggs. Some just lay one or two in a season, like a morepork, others, like the Californian quail, can lay up to 20 eggs.

SHELL The egg's hard shell has tiny pores (holes) that let the embryo breath.

EMBRYO The scientific name for the growing baby bird in the egg.

ALBUMEN Also known as egg white, it provides protection for the embryo and yolk.

YOLK This is what feeds the embryo.

ANATOMY OF AN EGG

When it's big enough, the chick breaks out of its shell. It has a special hard tip on its beak called an 'egg tooth' which helps it break out and hatch. This tooth disappears as the chick grows.

Most chicks are blind, bald and helpless when they are born. They need their parents to feed them and keep them warm.

BLACKBIRD

Since its release into New Zealand in 1862, the blackbird has spread to live all over Aotearoa, easily adapting to many different environments.

It seems there is almost always a beady-eyed blackbird or two watching your activities in the garden. They are not shy, and will hop right up and grab a worm or grub as you turn the soil in the veggie garden.

Males are jet black with a yellow bill and yellow eye-ring, while females are dark brown with light brown around the throat.

You often hear their 'cluck, cluck, cluck' alarm call as they take to the wing. Maybe they've spotted a cat lurking in the bushes!

HOUSE
SPARROW

The house sparrow is one of the world's most successful introduced species. It can adapt to all kinds of climates and so is found in almost every country on Earth. In Aotearoa, it is the most common bird found in the garden.

The sparrow's nesting site and food sources are almost always close to where humans live. Have a look around the roof and gutters of your house and more than likely you'll find a community of noisy sparrows nesting.

Sparrows have a strong, triangular beak typical of grain feeders. Males are bright brown and black and white. The female sparrows and young birds are pale brown and grey. They have a repetitive, monotonous call that goes 'cheep, cheep, cheep'.

STARLING

The starling is one of the most common birds you'll see in your backyard. Starlings were introduced from Europe in the 1860s to control caterpillar plagues on crops.

A starling has spectacular breeding plumage, with glossy black, green and purple iridescent colours. This means it shimmers in different lights.

In certain parts of the country, starlings can form massive pre-roosting flocks called a murmuration. In Europe, these flocks can reach into the millions.

You will often see groups of starlings jabbing their sharp, pointed beaks into the lawn, in search of invertebrates such as grass grubs and worms.

SONG THRUSH

The song thrush was introduced from Europe around the same time as the starling. As the name suggests, the thrush is one of the most recognisable songsters found in the garden. They're often heard singing high in a tree, on top of a roof or on a power pole.

The song thrush can be easily confused with a female blackbird, being a similar size and brown colour. But you can tell the thrush apart by its breast feathers, which are cream coloured with dark brown spots.

It feeds mainly on the ground, hopping and then stopping abruptly to stand motionless. It's looking mainly for invertebrates like worms, spiders, millipedes, but if it finds a snail, it will smash it open on a stone or a concrete path. It will return to use the same rock or hard surface over and over.

PĪWAKAWAKA
FANTAIL

Probably the most recognised and loved native bird, the pīwakawaka is not shy to swoop and loop in close to us, all the while joyfully chattering and squeaking.

Most pīwakawaka are pied in colour, which means having patches of one or two colours, but there is also a small population that is all black. These black pīwakawaka are found mostly in the South Island.

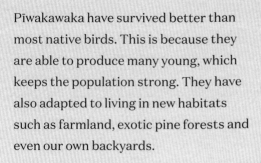

Pīwakawaka have survived better than most native birds. This is because they are able to produce many young, which keeps the population strong. They have also adapted to living in new habitats such as farmland, exotic pine forests and even our own backyards.

They feed almost exclusively on insects, using their fan-shaped tail to deftly flit in the air, catching small flying insects such as gnats, sandflies and moths.

SILVEREYE
TAUHOU

Named silvereye or waxeye because of its distinctive white ring around its eye, its Māori name, tauhou, means stranger. They found their way here from Australia in 1832, when a flock is believed to have been swept across the Tasman Sea in a storm. Because there is no evidence that it was introduced by humans, it is classified as a native bird and given the same protection.

It is now found in large numbers all over New Zealand in a wide range of habitats: native forest, scrub, plantations, rural and urban orchards and gardens. In winter, they form chattering flocks and move about in search of invertebrates (animals without a backbone), as well as fruit and nectar.

Their nests are finely woven cups, mostly built high up in small branches of shrubs or trees. Two to five pale-blue eggs can be found in each nest.

KERERŪ

A kererū shows little fear of humans and can be approached easily. This fearlessness made its pure white chest an easy target for early Māori and settlers, who prized these plump birds as a food source.

It is a strong flyer with a familiar '*swoosh swoosh*' sound that it makes with its beating wings.

Occasionally, it gorges so heavily on ripe fruit that it becomes very full (or 'drunk') and has been known to fall out of trees.

It can travel long distances to find ripe native fruit and kōwhai flowers. The kererū is an important seed distributor. It is one of the only New Zealand birds that eats the whole fruit, then it drops the seeds that are in its poo onto the forest floor.

KŌTARE
KINGFISHER

The kōtare/kingfisher can often be seen near water, perched up on a wire, on top of a lamp post or any other good spot to spy on potential prey. You might hear their characteristic high-pitched call: '*kek-kek-kek*'.

It can also be found in a wide variety of environments, from freshwater or estuaries, to open country. It hunts small prey such as insects, crabs, tadpoles and fish, to larger prey like lizards, mice and even birds.

As the bird does risky dives into water to catch small fish or tadpoles, a semi-transparent membrane is drawn across its eyes to help protect it.

Kōtare have been recorded diving a metre into water to take their prey.

RURU MOREPORK

Ruru/morepork are New Zealand's only surviving native owl. A similar species can be found in Australia called a boobook. You can hear the ruru's two-part calls start up in the evenings. Early Pākehā settlers named it 'more-pork' because that's how they thought its call sounded.

Like other owls, it has serrated or comb-like edges to its flight feathers, which gives it the ability to hunt in total silence.

The ruru catches and feeds on a variety of prey, including large insects like huhu beetles, wētā and moths, small birds, and even mice and young rats.

TŪĪ

The beautiful tūī is one of the most common native birds that you might find in your garden. It has short wide wings. The loud whirring noise the wings make can chase other birds away. They can also easily fly through dense forest.

There is a wide range of tuneful melodies a tūī sings as well as strange clicks and whistles and grunts. They actually have two voice boxes that allows them to sing ultrasonic notes, which are out of our hearing range. They mimic other birds and even human sounds like a cell phone!

The tūī dips its curved beak into flowers and curls its brush-tipped tongue into the nectar of flax/harakeke, kōwhai, rewarewa and other flowering natives. Sometimes you might see its forehead smudged with pollen. The pollen is then transferred to the next plant the tūī moves to. In this way, it pollinates the plant and helps it to survive.

WELCOME SWALLOW
WAROU

Warou/welcome swallows are most commonly seen near waterways. These little birds dart and swoop as they feed on the wing, picking flying insects out of the air or from the surface of the water. Another bird that came from Australia, they were first recorded in Northland in 1958. Now they are found in almost all parts of the country.

Some common places you may spot their nests are under bridges or jetties, under the eaves of a house or in the mouth of a cave. Once their nest, shaped out of mud and grass, has been constructed, it can be reused year after year.

When swallows hunt on the wing it's called 'hawking'. Swallows also drink in flight by scooping up a beakful from a river or stream.

RIRORIRO
GREY WARBLER

This native bird is found throughout the country and in good numbers. The riroriro/grey warbler is happy to move into urban areas close to where humans live. It is a tiny songbird that usually keeps well hidden in dense canopy at the top of trees.

It is most often heard rather than seen. For a tiny bird it has a big voice that carries quite far, letting you know it's in the garden.

The riroriro weighs up to 6 grams, making it one of Aotearoa's smallest birds. It is also known for its ability as a foster parent. Often a pīpīwharauroa/shining cuckoo will lay a single egg into the riroriro's own nest. When the cuckoo chick hatches, it clears out the riroriro's eggs, or even chicks, and the rirorio parents then raise the much-larger cuckoo chick as their own.

KORIMAKO
BELLBIRD

The korimako/bellbird is widespread throughout much of New Zealand, except for Auckland and Northland where it is rare on the mainland. No one is sure why this is.

The korimako has a beautiful song, which sounds very similar to a tūī. Although the tūī and korimako look very different, they are part of the same family of honeyeaters, both with curved bills and brush tongues designed for a nectar diet.

A korimako may visit gardens in spring, on the hunt for flowering plants, or in late summer for ripe fruit. Chicks are fed on insects and spiders collected for them by their parents.

WEKA

Weka are now only found in limited areas of mainland New Zealand. In recent years, they have migrated from the Marlborough Sounds and found a new home in the Nelson region, often seen in people's backyards. Weka are cheeky omnivores (eats plants and animals). They will steal food from a veggie patch, but they've even be known to sneak through an open back door and raid the pantry for goodies!

KĀKĀ

In the suburbs surrounding Zealandia, the wildlife sanctuary in Wellington, people are now familiar with kākā. These raucous parrots screech and squawk as they joyously wheel overhead. They can even be heard in the night, getting up to mysterious nocturnal activities.

PŪKEKO

People living in rural areas will be familiar with pūkeko, which can be seen foraging in paddocks and along roadsides. When disturbed, they prefer to run or hide rather than fly. Despite not having webbed feet, they are also strong swimmers.

FINCHES

Finches are small birds with short, strong, triangular-shaped beaks designed for cracking open seeds. Mostly they only have a seed diet, but sometimes they are known to eat small invertebrates. Aotearoa has no native finches. The four finch species were all introduced from Europe in the 1860s.

GOLDFINCH These brightly coloured finches are easy to spot, with their red face patches and bars of intense yellow on the wing. Gardeners like them around because the goldfinch feeds mostly on the seeds of weeds such as thistles, and pest insects like aphids.

CHAFFINCH Once introduced, the chaffinch quickly became a problem with grain farmers around South Canterbury and other grain-growing areas. The crop damage became so bad that money or a 'bounty' was paid out for dead chaffinches, to lower their numbers.

GREENFINCH These can be seen in large flocks. They are olive-green birds with flashes of yellow on the wings. Like the chaffinch, they are a serious problem to seed-crop farmers.

REDPOLL This is the smallest finch and the one you would probably see the least, unless in hill country. Redpolls have a red forehead, and males also have a bright crimson breast during the breeding season. The nest is a small untidy cup of fine twigs and grass, lined with feathers and hair.

MAGPIE

Magpies were introduced from Australia in 1874 to help control pests on farmland. They've since become very common, and in some parts of the country even considered a pest themselves. These big, handsome black and white birds strut about in local parks and sports fields.

They use their strong, dagger-like bill to prise earthworms or grubs out of the ground, but they're not fussy eaters and will happily feed on whatever they find, be it fruit, lizards, mice, other birds' eggs or chicks.

They are well known for being fiercely protective of their nesting sites. Being a highly intelligent bird, they can remember the face of an offender who has previously trespassed on their territory and might dive bomb them!

CALIFORNIA QUAIL

The California quail was released into New Zealand in the 1860s as a game bird for hunting. It can now be found in most parts of the country.

This male is on watch, high on a roof. If a predator is spotted, he makes an alarm call. Coveys (a flock of quails) will then dash or flutter into dense bushes or scrub.

The plume or top-knot is less obvious on the female, and her plumage is more camouflaged, which makes her harder for predators to find when she's sitting on her eggs. The female lays very large clutches of up to 20 eggs, because many of the chicks won't survive.

Ground birds like quail need to be able to escape predators from a very early age, and so within 24 hours of hatching, the chicks are ready to leave the nest, and within 10 days are able to fly. They can't fly well, but good enough to escape to cover.

MYNA

If you live in the top half of the North Island, you'll be familiar with this handsome but harsh, noisy bird. The myna is a tropical bird introduced from South Asia in the 1870s to help control insect crop pests, but as is often the case with introduced species, now they cause more harm than good.

They gather in large flocks to feed on food crops or fruit. Mynas are often seen along the road, seeking road-killed insects, they find food scraps at refuse dumps in winter, and flock onto paddocks being ploughed.

The myna aggressively defends its nesting site, pushing out native species, sometimes even destroying the eggs or chicks found in a nest, and taking over. It's not really understood why, but when introduced to other countries like New Zealand, they lose their musical ability, and are limited mostly to just harsh squawks and screeches.

EASTERN ROSELLA

Rosella were once household pets kept in cages, which have since escaped and formed wild populations. There is only a small population of rosella in the South Island, around Dunedin. The majority is found in the North Island.

These multi-coloured birds really stand out with their dazzling rainbow plumage. They are shy of people and will quickly take to the wing if disturbed.

Even though they look beautiful, escaped pet birds can compete with native birds for food and they also risk spreading foreign diseases and parasites.

ROCK PIGEON

Introduced into Aotearoa by early settlers for food and to keep as pets, the rock pigeon was also used to carry messages between towns, and for racing competitions. Even now, there are clubs that race pigeons.

Rock pigeons have extraordinary abilities – they can be taught to navigate between locations and some flights during races have been recorded at over 2700 kilometres.

Originally at home in sea cliffs and rock ledges, pigeons have adapted to city life. They now roost and breed on ledges and in crevices of buildings. City pigeons can cause problems, though, by spreading disease-causing bacteria in their poo, such as salmonella.

DUNNOCK

Also known as the hedge sparrow, the dunnock is common throughout the country, except in the top of the North Island.

These birds can be confused with a female house sparrow, both being a drab brown colour, but house sparrows are larger than a dunnock, with stronger triangular beaks.

Their diet is mainly small invertebrates such as beetles, flies, ants and spiders. Adults often feed nestlings with much-larger insect prey, for example, a moth up to 10 times bigger than their bill.

YELLOWHAMMER

Introduced from Britain in the 1860s, the songs that yellowhammers sing here in Aotearoa appear to have now been lost in their homeland.

Yellowhammers are similar in body size to a house sparrow; however, their tail is longer. They are frequently seen feeding on the seeds in hay fed to livestock. Flocks may cause much loss of newly sown grass seed on lawns and playing fields and in parks.

ATTRACTING NATIVE BIRDS

There are some simple ways to attract more native birds into your garden. The easiest way is by providing food that native birds love. Winter and early spring is a great time to feed them because that's when their food is scarce.

Tūī, korimako/bellbird and other nectar-feeding birds will enjoy a dish of sugar water. To make a sugar solution, dissolve half a cup of sugar in four cups of water. Don't add too much sugar or wasps may want to share it.

Nailing some bits of fresh fruit to the fence is a simple way to attach native birds such as kererū, tūī, and in some parts of New Zealand like Wellington, even kākā.

Try making a coconut feeder. Carefully cut away a quarter of a coconut with a saw. Drill a hole in the top for the string and tie it to a branch. You can also put bits of fruit inside.

In the summer months, a bird bath or a shallow tray of water gives birds a place to drink and clean. Native birds prefer to bathe off the ground, perhaps on a table or fence, but make sure cats cannot get to it.

You could also look at the plants in your garden and think about the ones that will encourage native birds to arrive in your backyard. Karamū, a fast-growing native shrub, kākā beak, a small tree with bright red hanging flowers, kōwhai trees for the tūī, and harakeke/flax are a few that native birds will love.

Allow leaf litter to build up under trees. This will encourage lots of insects, which will then provide a meal for many species of native birds.

Karori, where we live, has a fantastic bird life – healthy numbers of pīwakawaka, tūī, riroriro, kererū and kōtare. And because we are near Zealandia wildlife sanctuary, we even have visits from kākā, kākāriki and korimako. Many beautiful introduced birds also appear, such as greenfinch, goldfinch, chaffinches and even rosella.

My eldest son, Rory, was fascinated with all things bird when he was young. One activity we got involved in was capturing garden birds in a 'mist net' with a local birding group. The birds were then banded, to keep track of their numbers, and released. This was when I had the idea for this book and it gave me a good knowledge of the species to cover. It was an incredible experience untangling tiny silvereyes and goldfinches from the net, holding a fragile, feathered creature and feeling its rapid heartbeats in my fingers.

Ned Barraud

Other titles by the author:

'Explore and Discover' series
Animals of Aotearoa
New Zealand's Backyard Beasts
Moonman
Watch out for the Weka
Tohorā: the southern right whale
Rockpools: a Guide for Kiwi Kids
Where is it?
What happened to the moa
Incredible Journeys